I'M DOING MY BEST

KNOCK KNOCK®
VENICE, CALIFORNIA

Created and published by Knock Knock
1635-B Electric Ave.
Venice, CA 90291
knockknockstuff.com

ISBN: 978-160106684-8
UPC: 825703-50080-6

20 19 18 17 16 15 14 13 12 11 10 9 8 7 6 5

YOU WANT
TO BE BETTER

And God knows, you're really trying. So why does it still feel hard? Should it really be *that* tough? Perhaps you were finally going to improve your leadership skills. Or was it a weight-loss program? A new fitness regime? No, wait—you were going to stop procrastinating. Get better at guitar?

Whatever your goal, you are embarking on a time-honored tradition; people have been trying to improve themselves since the world began. In the fourth century BC the great Greek orator Demosthenes corrected his speech impediment by reciting with stones in his mouth. What are the odds he swallowed a few stones and thought about becoming a shepherd?

As long as people have been trying to better themselves, they've faced doubts, setbacks, and failure. While most of us do this anonymously, others have hit roadblocks quite famously. Orville and Wilbur Wright watched a lot of plane crashes before they took off. Twenty-seven publishers turned down Dr. Seuss's first book. Steve Jobs was fired from the company he created. Michael Jordan was cut from his high school basketball team. J. K. Rowling was a broke single mom when she created Harry Potter.

The key to moving beyond setbacks in your quest for self-improvement is resilience. Take stock, correct the problem, learn from it, and keep moving. *Psychology Today* puts it clearly: "There are some common traits among individuals who quickly move past failure and indeed benefit from it. They are able to step back and evaluate their failure. . . . They do not become paralyzed by their failed experience."

Whenever you overcome a setback, you'll build confidence that you'll be able to start fresh, again and again, if you need to. Journaling will help you see that progression. If you eat your weight in potato chips or yell at your kids, you can record the lapse, how you responded, and how you moved on.

In addition to helping you keep track of your self-improvement hiccups, journal writing has been shown to have many powerful benefits. As noted self-help guru Deepak Chopra claims, "Journaling is one of the most powerful tools we have to transform our lives," and there is consistent evidence that journal writing aids physical health. According to a widely cited study by James W. Pennebaker and Janel D. Seagal, "Writing about important personal experiences in an emotional way . . . brings about improvements in mental and physical health." Proven benefits include better stress management, strengthened immune systems, fewer doctor visits, and improvement in chronic illnesses such as asthma.

It's not entirely clear how journaling accomplishes all this. Catharsis is involved, but many also point to the value of organizing experiences into a cohesive narrative. According to *Newsweek*, some experts believe that journaling "forces us to transform the ruminations cluttering our minds into coherent stories." When you write down each roadblock it becomes a story of how you met the challenge and overcame it.

As a devotee of this journal, you obviously have the self-awareness to be honest about your setbacks in the process of trying to reign in whatever needs reigning in, such as that out-of-control spending or plain old bitterness. To take advantage of the journaling process fully, however, don't simply vent about your failures. Instead, record them and then try to understand them.

Specialists agree that in order to reap the benefits of journaling you have to stick with it, quasi-daily, for as little as five minutes at a time (at least fifteen minutes, however, is best). Finding regular writing times and comfortable locations can help with consistency. If you can't think of where to start, use the quotes inside this journal as a jumping-off point for observations and explorations. Finally, determine a home for your journal where you can reference it when the self-improvement journey takes an untoward detour— like near the cookie jar or your credit card.

J. K. Rowling told Harvard's class of 2008, "It is impossible to live without failing at something, unless you live so cautiously that you might as well not have lived at all—in which case, you fail by default. . . . The knowledge that you have emerged wiser and stronger from setbacks means that you are, ever after, secure in your ability to survive." Take it from someone who persevered to make millions believe in magic and attempt to play Quidditch: embrace the setbacks, learn from them, and keep on trucking. Or, perhaps, just try something else altogether.

You may be
disappointed
if you fail, but
you are doomed
if you don't try.

Beverly Sills

HOW I'M WORKING ON MYSELF TODAY:

_____

_____

_____

_____

_____

_____

_____

_____

_____

_____

_____

_____

_____

_____

_____

_____

_____

TODAY'S PERSONAL OUTLOOK:

I'd do anything for a good body except exercise and eat right.

Steve Martin

DATE

HOW I'M WORKING ON MYSELF TODAY:

_____

_____

_____

_____

_____

_____

_____

_____

_____

_____

_____

_____

_____

_____

_____

TODAY'S PERSONAL OUTLOOK:

Real growth often happens
outside of where we intend it to,
in the interstitial spaces—what
Dr. Seuss calls "the waiting place."

Bruce Mau

DATE

HOW I'M WORKING ON MYSELF TODAY:

_____

_____

_____

_____

_____

_____

_____

_____

_____

_____

_____

_____

_____

_____

_____

_____

_____

_____

TODAY'S PERSONAL OUTLOOK:

In any case you
mustn't confuse
a single failure
with a final defeat.

F. Scott Fitzgerald

HOW I'M WORKING ON MYSELF TODAY:

_____

_____

_____

_____

_____

_____

_____

_____

_____

_____

_____

_____

_____

_____

_____

_____

_____

_____

TODAY'S PERSONAL OUTLOOK:

Even though you get the monkey off your back, the circus never really leaves town.

Anne Lamott

DATE

HOW I'M WORKING ON MYSELF TODAY:

_____

_____

_____

_____

_____

_____

_____

_____

_____

_____

_____

_____

_____

_____

_____

_____

_____

_____

TODAY'S PERSONAL OUTLOOK:

The brick walls are there for a reason. They're not there to keep us out. The brick walls are there to give us a chance to show how badly we want something.

Randy Pausch

DATE		

HOW I'M WORKING ON MYSELF TODAY:

_____

_____

_____

_____

_____

_____

_____

_____

_____

_____

_____

_____

_____

_____

_____

_____

_____

TODAY'S PERSONAL OUTLOOK:

If I had to live my life again, I'd make all the same mistakes, only sooner.

Tallulah Bankhead

DATE

HOW I'M WORKING ON MYSELF TODAY:

_____

_____

_____

_____

_____

_____

_____

_____

_____

_____

_____

_____

_____

_____

_____

_____

TODAY'S PERSONAL OUTLOOK:

She would be a new person,
she vowed. They said no matter
how far a mule travels it can
never come back a horse, but
she would show them all.

Junot Diaz

HOW I'M WORKING ON MYSELF TODAY:

TODAY'S PERSONAL OUTLOOK:

I really don't think
I need buns of steel.
I'd be happy with
buns of cinnamon.

Ellen DeGeneres

DATE

HOW I'M WORKING ON MYSELF TODAY:

_____

_____

_____

_____

_____

_____

_____

_____

_____

_____

_____

_____

_____

_____

_____

_____

_____

_____

TODAY'S PERSONAL OUTLOOK:

It's a good thing to have all the props pulled out from under us occasionally. It gives us some sense of what is rock under our feet, and what is sand.

Madeleine L'Engle

DATE

HOW I'M WORKING ON MYSELF TODAY:

_____

_____

_____

_____

_____

_____

_____

_____

_____

_____

_____

_____

_____

_____

_____

_____

_____

_____

TODAY'S PERSONAL OUTLOOK:

There's only one corner of the universe you can be certain of improving, and that's your own self.

Aldous Huxley

HOW I'M WORKING ON MYSELF TODAY:

_____

_____

_____

_____

_____

_____

_____

_____

_____

_____

_____

_____

_____

_____

_____

_____

_____

_____

TODAY'S PERSONAL OUTLOOK:

Every day is a new beginning and a chance to blow it.

Cathy Guisewite

HOW I'M WORKING ON MYSELF TODAY:

_____
_____
_____
_____
_____
_____
_____
_____
_____
_____
_____
_____
_____
_____
_____
_____
_____
_____
_____

TODAY'S PERSONAL OUTLOOK:

You can't turn a sow's ear into veal Orloff, but you can do something very good with a sow's ear.

Julia Child

HOW I'M WORKING ON MYSELF TODAY:

_____

_____

_____

_____

_____

_____

_____

_____

_____

_____

_____

_____

_____

_____

_____

_____

_____

_____

TODAY'S PERSONAL OUTLOOK:

I suppose it is tempting, if the only tool you have is a hammer, to treat everything as if it were a nail.

Abraham Maslow

DATE

HOW I'M WORKING ON MYSELF TODAY:

_____

_____

_____

_____

_____

_____

_____

_____

_____

_____

_____

_____

_____

_____

_____

_____

_____

TODAY'S PERSONAL OUTLOOK:

Woe-is-me is not an attractive narrative.

Maureen Dowd

DATE

HOW I'M WORKING ON MYSELF TODAY:

_____

_____

_____

_____

_____

_____

_____

_____

_____

_____

_____

_____

_____

_____

_____

_____

TODAY'S PERSONAL OUTLOOK:

It is a common experience that a problem difficult at night is resolved in the morning after the committee of sleep has worked on it.

John Steinbeck

DATE

HOW I'M WORKING ON MYSELF TODAY:

_____

_____

_____

_____

_____

_____

_____

_____

_____

_____

_____

_____

_____

_____

_____

_____

_____

TODAY'S PERSONAL OUTLOOK:

The need for change bulldozed a road down the center of my mind.

Maya Angelou

DATE

HOW I'M WORKING ON MYSELF TODAY:

_____

_____

_____

_____

_____

_____

_____

_____

_____

_____

_____

_____

_____

_____

_____

_____

_____

TODAY'S PERSONAL OUTLOOK:

A quilt may take a year, but if you just keep doing it, you get a quilt.

Chuck Close

DATE

HOW I'M WORKING ON MYSELF TODAY:

_____

_____

_____

_____

_____

_____

_____

_____

_____

_____

_____

_____

_____

_____

_____

_____

_____

_____

TODAY'S PERSONAL OUTLOOK:

All life is an experiment. . . .
What if you do fail, and get fairly
rolled in the dirt once or twice?
Up again, you shall never be so
afraid of a tumble.

Ralph Waldo Emerson

HOW I'M WORKING ON MYSELF TODAY:

_____

_____

_____

_____

_____

_____

_____

_____

_____

_____

_____

_____

_____

_____

_____

_____

_____

_____

TODAY'S PERSONAL OUTLOOK:

Diets are not there to be picked and mixed but picked and stuck to, which is exactly what I shall begin to do once I've eaten this chocolate croissant.

Helen Fielding

HOW I'M WORKING ON MYSELF TODAY:

_____

_____

_____

_____

_____

_____

_____

_____

_____

_____

_____

_____

_____

_____

_____

_____

_____

_____

TODAY'S PERSONAL OUTLOOK:

If you want to slip into a round hole, you must make a ball of yourself.

George Eliot

HOW I'M WORKING ON MYSELF TODAY:

_____

_____

_____

_____

_____

_____

_____

_____

_____

_____

_____

_____

_____

_____

_____

_____

_____

TODAY'S PERSONAL OUTLOOK:

Whenever I go on a ride, I'm always thinking of what's wrong with the thing and how it can be improved.

Walt Disney

HOW I'M WORKING ON MYSELF TODAY:

_____

_____

_____

_____

_____

_____

_____

_____

_____

_____

_____

_____

_____

_____

_____

_____

_____

TODAY'S PERSONAL OUTLOOK:

A problem is a chance for you
to do your best.

Duke Ellington

DATE

HOW I'M WORKING ON MYSELF TODAY:

_____

_____

_____

_____

_____

_____

_____

_____

_____

_____

_____

_____

_____

_____

_____

_____

_____

TODAY'S PERSONAL OUTLOOK:

Ever tried.
Ever failed.
No matter.
Try again.
Fail again.
Fail better.

Samuel Beckett

DATE

HOW I'M WORKING ON MYSELF TODAY:

_____

_____

_____

_____

_____

_____

_____

_____

_____

_____

_____

_____

_____

_____

_____

_____

_____

_____

TODAY'S PERSONAL OUTLOOK:

The slogan "press on" has solved and always will solve the problems of the human race.

Calvin Coolidge

HOW I'M WORKING ON MYSELF TODAY:

_____
_____
_____
_____
_____
_____
_____
_____
_____
_____
_____
_____
_____
_____
_____
_____
_____

TODAY'S PERSONAL OUTLOOK:

The problem with self-improvement is knowing when to quit.

David Lee Roth

HOW I'M WORKING ON MYSELF TODAY:

_____

_____

_____

_____

_____

_____

_____

_____

_____

_____

_____

_____

_____

_____

_____

_____

TODAY'S PERSONAL OUTLOOK:

Talent is insignificant.
I know a lot of talented
ruins. Beyond talent lie
all the usual words:
discipline, love, luck, but,
most of all, endurance.

James Baldwin

HOW I'M WORKING ON MYSELF TODAY:

_____

_____

_____

_____

_____

_____

_____

_____

_____

_____

_____

_____

_____

_____

_____

_____

_____

TODAY'S PERSONAL OUTLOOK:

I think I'm the happiest I've ever been. Part of it is just learning what makes me happier and doing more of it, and learning what makes me unhappier and doing less of it.

Mark Frauenfelder

DATE

HOW I'M WORKING ON MYSELF TODAY:

_____

_____

_____

_____

_____

_____

_____

_____

_____

_____

_____

_____

_____

_____

_____

_____

_____

_____

TODAY'S PERSONAL OUTLOOK:

When all else fails, you always have delusion.

Conan O'Brien

DATE

HOW I'M WORKING ON MYSELF TODAY:

You can't be that kid standing at the top of the waterslide, overthinking it. You have to go down the chute.

Tina Fey

DATE

HOW I'M WORKING ON MYSELF TODAY:

_____

_____

_____

_____

_____

_____

_____

_____

_____

_____

_____

_____

_____

_____

_____

_____

_____

TODAY'S PERSONAL OUTLOOK:

It's our choices, Harry, that show what we truly are, far more than our abilities.

J. K. Rowling

DATE

HOW I'M WORKING ON MYSELF TODAY:

_____

_____

_____

_____

_____

_____

_____

_____

_____

_____

_____

_____

_____

_____

_____

_____

_____

_____

TODAY'S PERSONAL OUTLOOK:

When you reach for
the stars, you may
not quite get them,
but you won't come
up with a handful
of mud either.

Leo Burnett

HOW I'M WORKING ON MYSELF TODAY:

_____

_____

_____

_____

_____

_____

_____

_____

_____

_____

_____

_____

_____

_____

_____

_____

TODAY'S PERSONAL OUTLOOK:

Every new adjustment is a crisis in self-esteem.

Eric Hoffer

DATE

HOW I'M WORKING ON MYSELF TODAY:

_____

_____

_____

_____

_____

_____

_____

_____

_____

_____

_____

_____

_____

_____

_____

_____

_____

_____

_____

_____

TODAY'S PERSONAL OUTLOOK:

I think somehow we learn who we really are and then live with that decision.

Eleanor Roosevelt

DATE

HOW I'M WORKING ON MYSELF TODAY:

_____

_____

_____

_____

_____

_____

_____

_____

_____

_____

_____

_____

_____

_____

_____

_____

_____

TODAY'S PERSONAL OUTLOOK:

Everybody has talent, and it's just a matter of moving around until you've discovered what it is.

George Lucas

DATE

HOW I'M WORKING ON MYSELF TODAY:

_____

_____

_____

_____

_____

_____

_____

_____

_____

_____

_____

_____

_____

_____

_____

_____

TODAY'S PERSONAL OUTLOOK:

The moment of change is the only poem.

Adrienne Rich

DATE

HOW I'M WORKING ON MYSELF TODAY:

_____

_____

_____

_____

_____

_____

_____

_____

_____

_____

_____

_____

_____

_____

_____

_____

_____

_____

TODAY'S PERSONAL OUTLOOK:

Sometimes I lie awake at night, and I ask, "Where have I gone wrong?" Then a voice says to me, "This is going to take more than one night."

Charles M. Schulz

DATE

HOW I'M WORKING ON MYSELF TODAY:

_____

_____

_____

_____

_____

_____

_____

_____

_____

_____

_____

_____

_____

_____

_____

_____

_____

TODAY'S PERSONAL OUTLOOK:

In the middle of the winter I learned at last that there was in me an invincible summer.

Albert Camus

HOW I'M WORKING ON MYSELF TODAY:

_____

_____

_____

_____

_____

_____

_____

_____

_____

_____

_____

_____

_____

_____

_____

_____

_____

_____

TODAY'S PERSONAL OUTLOOK:

Man is a nerve of the cosmos,
dislocated, trying to quiver
into place.

Jean Toomer

DATE

HOW I'M WORKING ON MYSELF TODAY:

Hope and change are hard-fought things.

Michelle Obama

HOW I'M WORKING ON MYSELF TODAY:

_____

_____

_____

_____

_____

_____

_____

_____

_____

_____

_____

_____

_____

_____

_____

_____

TODAY'S PERSONAL OUTLOOK:

My happiness grows in direct proportion to my acceptance and in inverse proportion to my expectations.

Michael J. Fox

DATE

HOW I'M WORKING ON MYSELF TODAY:

_____

_____

_____

_____

_____

_____

_____

_____

_____

_____

_____

_____

_____

_____

_____

_____

_____

TODAY'S PERSONAL OUTLOOK:

I think that anyone who's pushed
to do the very best that they can
is privileged. It's a luxury.

Twyla Tharp

HOW I'M WORKING ON MYSELF TODAY:

_____

_____

_____

_____

_____

_____

_____

_____

_____

_____

_____

_____

_____

_____

_____

_____

_____

TODAY'S PERSONAL OUTLOOK:

And the trouble is,
if you don't risk
anything, you
risk even *more*.

Erica Jong

DATE

HOW I'M WORKING ON MYSELF TODAY:

_____

_____

_____

_____

_____

_____

_____

_____

_____

_____

_____

_____

_____

_____

_____

_____

_____

_____

TODAY'S PERSONAL OUTLOOK:

Sometimes people let the same problem make them miserable for years when they could just say, "So what." That's one of my favorite things to say. "So what."

Andy Warhol

DATE

HOW I'M WORKING ON MYSELF TODAY:

The indispensable
first step to getting
the things you want
out of life is this:
Decide what
you want.

Ben Stein

DATE

HOW I'M WORKING ON MYSELF TODAY:

_____

_____

_____

_____

_____

_____

_____

_____

_____

_____

_____

_____

_____

_____

_____

_____

_____

_____

TODAY'S PERSONAL OUTLOOK:

**ABSTAINER, n.
A weak person who
yields to the temptation
of denying himself
a pleasure.**

Ambrose Bierce

HOW I'M WORKING ON MYSELF TODAY:

_____

_____

_____

_____

_____

_____

_____

_____

_____

_____

_____

_____

_____

_____

_____

_____

TODAY'S PERSONAL OUTLOOK:

One setback is one setback—it is not the end of the world.

Jillian Michaels

DATE

HOW I'M WORKING ON MYSELF TODAY:

_____

_____

_____

_____

_____

_____

_____

_____

_____

_____

_____

_____

_____

_____

_____

TODAY'S PERSONAL OUTLOOK:

The only thing that I have done that is not mitigated by luck, diminished by good fortune, is that I persisted. And other people gave up.

Harrison Ford

DATE

HOW I'M WORKING ON MYSELF TODAY:

By not trying we throw away the chance of an immense good; by not succeeding we only incur the loss of a little human labor.

Francis Bacon

DATE

HOW I'M WORKING ON MYSELF TODAY:

_____

_____

_____

_____

_____

_____

_____

_____

_____

_____

_____

_____

_____

_____

_____

_____

_____

TODAY'S PERSONAL OUTLOOK:

A sobering thought:
what if, at this very
moment, I am living
up to my full potential?

Jane Wagner

DATE		

HOW I'M WORKING ON MYSELF TODAY:

_____

_____

_____

_____

_____

_____

_____

_____

_____

_____

_____

_____

_____

_____

_____

_____

_____

TODAY'S PERSONAL OUTLOOK:

Like a fish which swims calmly in deep water, I felt all about me the secure supporting pressure of my own life. Ragged, inglorious, and apparently purposeless, but my own.

Iris Murdoch

HOW I'M WORKING ON MYSELF TODAY:

TODAY'S PERSONAL OUTLOOK:

We choose to
go to the moon
in this decade and
do the other things,
not because they are
easy, but because
they are hard.

John F. Kennedy

HOW I'M WORKING ON MYSELF TODAY:

_____

_____

_____

_____

_____

_____

_____

_____

_____

_____

_____

_____

_____

_____

_____

_____

_____

TODAY'S PERSONAL OUTLOOK:

As one gets older . . . one discovers that everything is always going to be exactly the same with different hats on.

Noël Coward

HOW I'M WORKING ON MYSELF TODAY:

_____

_____

_____

_____

_____

_____

_____

_____

_____

_____

_____

_____

_____

_____

_____

_____

_____

TODAY'S PERSONAL OUTLOOK:

You can settle for
reality, or you can go
off, like a fool, and
dream another dream.

Nora Ephron

HOW I'M WORKING ON MYSELF TODAY:

_____

_____

_____

_____

_____

_____

_____

_____

_____

_____

_____

_____

_____

_____

_____

_____

_____

_____

_____

TODAY'S PERSONAL OUTLOOK:

Blame someone else and get on with your life.

Alan Woods

DATE

HOW I'M WORKING ON MYSELF TODAY:

_____

_____

_____

_____

_____

_____

_____

_____

_____

_____

_____

_____

_____

_____

_____

_____

_____

TODAY'S PERSONAL OUTLOOK:

People wish to learn to swim and at the same time to keep one foot on the ground.

Marcel Proust

HOW I'M WORKING ON MYSELF TODAY:

TODAY'S PERSONAL OUTLOOK:

When asked, "How do you write?" I invariably answer, "One word at a time."

Stephen King

DATE

HOW I'M WORKING ON MYSELF TODAY:

_____

_____

_____

_____

_____

_____

_____

_____

_____

_____

_____

_____

_____

_____

_____

_____

_____

TODAY'S PERSONAL OUTLOOK:

Habit is overcome by habit.

Desiderius Erasmus

HOW I'M WORKING ON MYSELF TODAY:

_____

_____

_____

_____

_____

_____

_____

_____

_____

_____

_____

_____

_____

_____

_____

_____

TODAY'S PERSONAL OUTLOOK:

Failure is not our only punishment for laziness; there is also the success of others.

Jules Renard

HOW I'M WORKING ON MYSELF TODAY:

_____

_____

_____

_____

_____

_____

_____

_____

_____

_____

_____

_____

_____

_____

_____

_____

TODAY'S PERSONAL OUTLOOK:

When we lose twenty pounds . . .
we may be losing the twenty best
pounds we have! We may be losing
the pounds that contain our genius,
our humanity, our love and honesty.

Woody Allen

HOW I'M WORKING ON MYSELF TODAY:

_____

_____

_____

_____

_____

_____

_____

_____

_____

_____

_____

_____

_____

_____

_____

_____

_____

_____

TODAY'S PERSONAL OUTLOOK:

Like anyone else,
she must have wanted
different things at the
same time. The human
heart is a dark forest.

Tobias Wolff

DATE

HOW I'M WORKING ON MYSELF TODAY:

_____

_____

_____

_____

_____

_____

_____

_____

_____

_____

_____

_____

_____

_____

_____

_____

_____

_____

TODAY'S PERSONAL OUTLOOK:

The triumph of anything is a matter of organization. If there are such things as angels, I hope that they are organized along the lines of the Mafia.

Kurt Vonnegut

DATE

HOW I'M WORKING ON MYSELF TODAY:

_____

_____

_____

_____

_____

_____

_____

_____

_____

_____

_____

_____

_____

_____

_____

_____

_____

TODAY'S PERSONAL OUTLOOK:

Achieving a goal is nothing. The getting there is everything.

Jules Michelet

DATE

HOW I'M WORKING ON MYSELF TODAY:

_____

_____

_____

_____

_____

_____

_____

_____

_____

_____

_____

_____

_____

_____

_____

_____

_____

TODAY'S PERSONAL OUTLOOK:

Discipline should not be practiced like a rule imposed on oneself from the outside, but that it becomes an expression of one's own will; that it is felt as pleasant, and that one slowly accustoms oneself to a kind of behavior which one would eventually miss, if one stopped practicing it.

Erich Fromm

DATE

HOW I'M WORKING ON MYSELF TODAY:

_____

_____

_____

_____

_____

_____

_____

_____

_____

_____

_____

_____

_____

_____

_____

_____

_____

TODAY'S PERSONAL OUTLOOK:

If you don't place
your foot on the rope,
you'll never cross
the chasm.

Liz Smith

HOW I'M WORKING ON MYSELF TODAY:

_____

_____

_____

_____

_____

_____

_____

_____

_____

_____

_____

_____

_____

_____

_____

_____

_____

_____

TODAY'S PERSONAL OUTLOOK:

Birthday resolution: From now on specialize; never again make any concession to the ninety-nine parts of you which are like everybody else at the expense of the one which is unique.

Cyril Connolly

DATE

HOW I'M WORKING ON MYSELF TODAY:

Poor me. There's nothing so sweet as wallowing in it is there? Wallowing is sex for depressives.

Jeanette Winterson

HOW I'M WORKING ON MYSELF TODAY:

_____

_____

_____

_____

_____

_____

_____

_____

_____

_____

_____

_____

_____

_____

_____

_____

_____

_____

TODAY'S PERSONAL OUTLOOK:

Anyone can have an off decade.

Larry Cole

	DATE	

HOW I'M WORKING ON MYSELF TODAY:

_____

_____

_____

_____

_____

_____

_____

_____

_____

_____

_____

_____

_____

_____

_____

_____

TODAY'S PERSONAL OUTLOOK:

Clinging to the past is the problem. Embracing change is the solution.

Gloria Steinem

HOW I'M WORKING ON MYSELF TODAY:

_____

_____

_____

_____

_____

_____

_____

_____

_____

_____

_____

_____

_____

_____

_____

_____

_____

TODAY'S PERSONAL OUTLOOK:

Experience is the name everyone gives to their mistakes.

Oscar Wilde

HOW I'M WORKING ON MYSELF TODAY:

_____

_____

_____

_____

_____

_____

_____

_____

_____

_____

_____

_____

_____

_____

_____

_____

_____

_____

TODAY'S PERSONAL OUTLOOK:

One must have chaos within
to enable one to give birth
to a dancing star.

Friedrich Nietzsche

DATE

HOW I'M WORKING ON MYSELF TODAY:

_____

_____

_____

_____

_____

_____

_____

_____

_____

_____

_____

_____

_____

_____

_____

_____

_____

_____

TODAY'S PERSONAL OUTLOOK:

I do the very best I know how—the very best I can; and I mean to keep on doing so until the end.

Abraham Lincoln

HOW I'M WORKING ON MYSELF TODAY:

_____

_____

_____

_____

_____

_____

_____

_____

_____

_____

_____

_____

_____

_____

_____

_____

TODAY'S PERSONAL OUTLOOK:

I made no resolutions for the
New Year. The habit of making
plans, of criticizing, sanctioning
and molding my life, is too much
of a daily event for me.

Anaïs Nin

HOW I'M WORKING ON MYSELF TODAY:

_____

_____

_____

_____

_____

_____

_____

_____

_____

_____

_____

_____

_____

_____

_____

_____

_____

TODAY'S PERSONAL OUTLOOK:

Knowing what you cannot do is more important than knowing what you can do. In fact, that's good taste.

Lucille Ball

HOW I'M WORKING ON MYSELF TODAY:

_____

_____

_____

_____

_____

_____

_____

_____

_____

_____

_____

_____

_____

_____

_____

_____

_____

_____

TODAY'S PERSONAL OUTLOOK:

Let us cultivate our garden.

Voltaire

DATE

HOW I'M WORKING ON MYSELF TODAY:

_____

_____

_____

_____

_____

_____

_____

_____

_____

_____

_____

_____

_____

_____

_____

_____

TODAY'S PERSONAL OUTLOOK:

She hoped to be wise
and reasonable in time;
but alas! alas! she must
confess to herself that
she was not wise yet.

Jane Austen

DATE

HOW I'M WORKING ON MYSELF TODAY:

_____

_____

_____

_____

_____

_____

_____

_____

_____

_____

_____

_____

_____

_____

_____

_____

TODAY'S PERSONAL OUTLOOK:

After all, tomorrow is another day.

Margaret Mitchell

DATE

HOW I'M WORKING ON MYSELF TODAY:

_____

_____

_____

_____

_____

_____

_____

_____

_____

_____

_____

_____

_____

_____

_____

_____

_____

TODAY'S PERSONAL OUTLOOK:

Keep your chin up.

Knock Knock